MW01714678

In the Sea

by Alex Plisky

HOUGHTON MIFFLIN BOSTON

PHOTOGRAPHY CREDITS: Cover © Martin Strmiska/Alamy; 1 © Jupiter Images/Polka Dot/Alamy: 2 © Jupiter Images/Comstock Images/Alamy; 3 © Martin Strmiska/Alamy; 4 © Philip Coblentz/Brand X/Corbis; 5 © Shutterstock; 6 © Robert Glusic/Corbis; 7 © Jupiter Images/Polka Dot/Alamy; 8 © Juice Drops; 9 © Jupiter Images/Creatas/Alamy; 10 © Shutterstock

Printed in China

ISBN-13: 978-0-547-02729-6
ISBN-10: 0-547-02729-X

16 17 18 19 0940 20 19 18 17
4500634148

A diver swims
under the sea.

Fish swim
in the water, too.

The diver swims
and looks.
She sees a stingray
on the sand.

A turtle swims by.
It uses its flippers
to swim in the sea.

The diver swims
and looks.
She sees starfish
on a rock.

A small crab tries to hide in a shell.

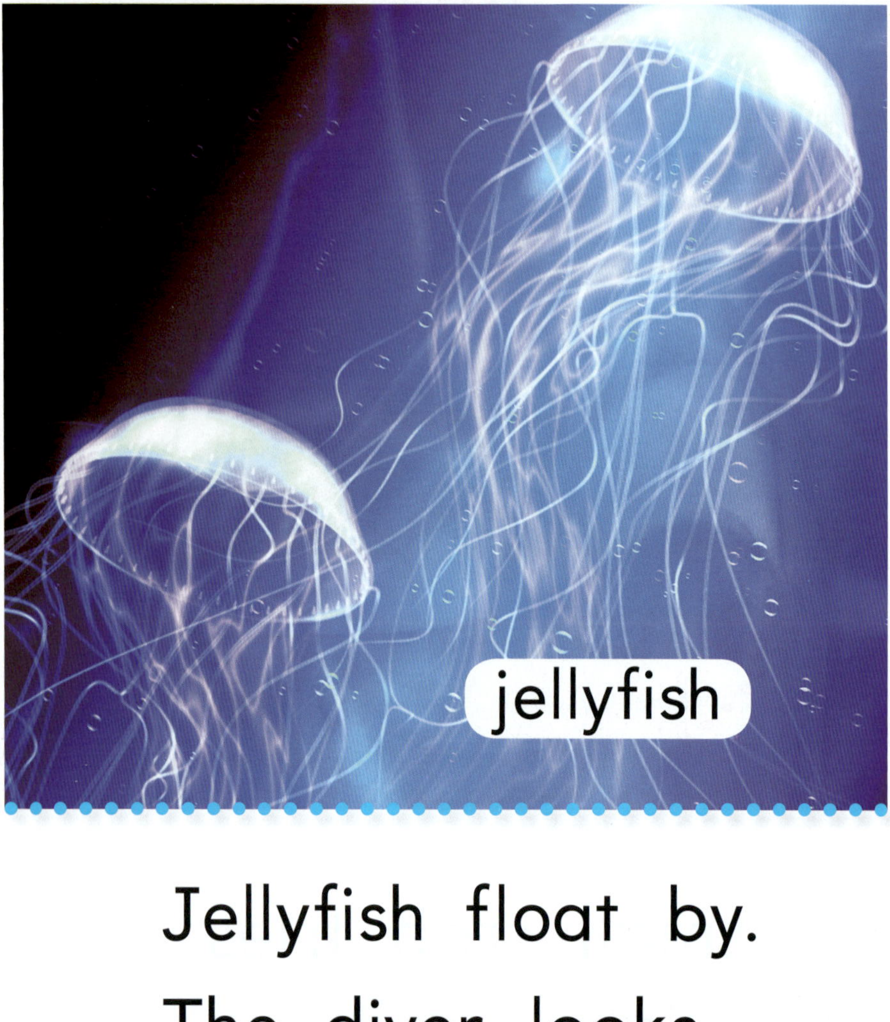

Jellyfish float by.
The diver looks
and swims away.

The diver swims
and looks.
She sees a dolphin
in the waves.

Click!
The dolphin smiles
for a picture!

Responding

TARGET SKILL Author's Purpose

Why did the author write this book? What are three details that tell you this? Make a chart.

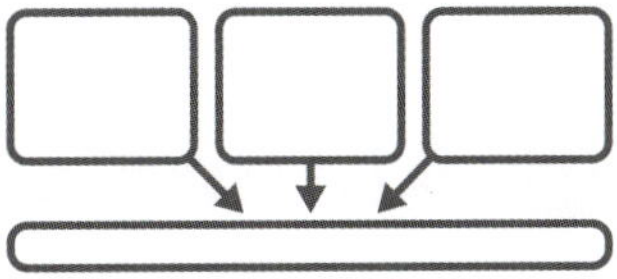

Talk About It

Text to Text Think of a different story about the ocean. What other kinds of animals live in the ocean?

WORDS TO KNOW

blue	live
cold	their
far	water
little	where

TARGET SKILL **Author's Purpose**

Tell why an author writes a book.

TARGET STRATEGY **Analyze/Evaluate**

Tell how you feel about the text, and why.

GENRE **Informational text** gives facts about a topic.